# Positive Posts
## FOR OCD & ANXIETY

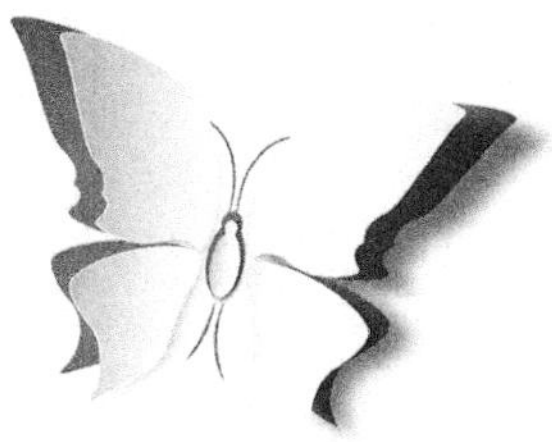

Help and Hope for
Those Who Need It Now

James Callner

ISBN: 978-0-9980729-2-0 (paperback)
ISBN: 978-0-9980729-3-7 (e-book)

Cover and interior designs and editing by Joanne Shwed, Backspace Ink (www.backspaceink.com)

Disclaimer: I am not a physician or a therapist but a person who has experienced modes of recovery for obsessive-compulsive disorder (OCD) for 38+ years. Everything you read in this book comes from my personal experience of recovery. I encourage you to discuss any method or technique with your own professional therapist, psychiatrist, or doctor.

To the courageous people in this world
who suffer from the very real disorders of
OCD and anxiety: Never ever give up hope
because there is hope. I am with you.

In gratitude:

Joanne Shwed
Brittany Tucker

Creative Consultants
Rachael Brown
Jeanine Sande
George Thibeault
Barbara Callner
Ron Wiebe

# What OCD Specialists and Peers Are Saying about *Positive Posts for OCD & Anxiety*

"I highly recommend Mr. Callner's new book *Positive Posts for OCD & Anxiety*. His understanding of OCD and anxiety is exceptional and the suggestions and guidance he offers in this book will help anyone suffering from OCD and anxiety on a daily basis."

— Sharon Davies, OCD Therapist and Director of The OCD Treatment Centre

"James Callner's work offers a common sense approach to the complicated problem of OCD. This book offers fuel for recovery, and a compassionate approach. He has helped me through some of the darkest of times."

— Mike Sizemore, OCD advocate Peer Support Specialist

"James Callner is one of the relatable peer support members of the OCD community because he is one of us. Jim is a retired college instructor who has written books and made many helpful videos on the subject of OCD. His latest book will be another useful tool for assisting us to manage our OCD."

— Richard Amato, founder of OCD Friends Support Group

"Amazing advice. Thank you so very much."

"Thanks so much, Jim! I really needed these motivational words today."

"OMG, thank you for this today. Jim. I needed to hear this!"

"Simply wonderful, James. Yes, we are highly sensitive people and we should remember to direct love inward more often."

"... your posts have always given me hope and the encouragement to keep going. I take a lot of your advice with regards to overcoming the disorder, which has helped me a great deal towards recovery."

— OCD Support Group members

# Contents

# About This Book

This book is designed so you can turn to any page for some understanding, guidance, and suggestions for recovery. I created this book for anyone who takes on OCD and anxiety every day—just like me.

# What Is ERP and CBT?

Exposure response prevention (ERP) therapy is still considered the gold standard therapy for OCD patients. Working with a trained ERP coach, ERP is about learning to face your fears without responding to them with compulsions or obsessions.

Cognitive behavioral therapy (CBT) is a directive therapy, which means that the therapist leads the process, teaching patients how to develop effective ways of coping with a range of problems including obsessions and compulsions.

# Positive Posts for OCD & Anxiety

What you are about to read is a collection of posts I created using online platforms some four years ago to today. When I retired after 37 years of teaching college, I decided to devote much of the rest of my life to helping those just like me. While recovering from OCD and anxiety since 1982, I have been fortunate to have some of the best psychiatrists, medical doctors, therapists, and spiritual teachers in the world. They all continue to be my teachers and mentors. I joined over 20 private and public online support groups and started posting my words of encouragement, strength, and hope. The posts in this book are some of the most popular ones and are appreciated by those in need of support, help, suggestions, and empathy. Sharing them with you is my greatest medicine.

— James Callner

You are far more than OCD. The general profile for someone with OCD is that they are intelligent, articulate, creative, highly sensitive, and empathetic.

# "What If"

Some call OCD the "what if" doubting disorder. "What if" has come to my mind more than any other question for most of my life.

"What if I get sick?"

"What if I get someone else sick?"

"What if that's contaminated?"

"What if I never get better?"

"What if the obsessive thoughts never stop?"

"What if I lose my job?"

The "what if" questions are endless because the nature of OCD is based on yearning for certainty that life can't provide in reality.

Here's another way to think about or work around the "what if" question: What if you changed up the question?

"What if I get sick but handle it?"

"What if I ask for support from my family, friends, or loved ones, and—if they don't give it—I ask a support group to help me?"

"What if I choose to find a job or keep my job no matter what?"

"What if I label the obsessions as OCD bullying and move on with my life anyway?"

"What if I have faith or trust that I can and will get better?"

"What if I ask for help, even if I don't feel like it?"

"What if I work at soothing myself?"

"What if I feel the feelings and do it anyway?"

So, what if we turned around the "what if" question to help others and ourselves?

*What if?*

"If a thought doesn't bring me inner peace, I don't follow it."

— Sharon Davies, OCD Therapist

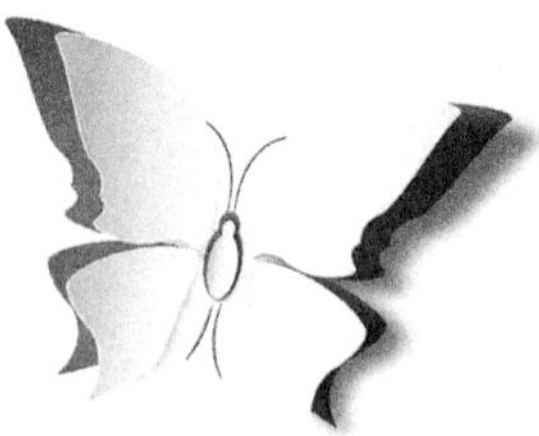

# Progress, Not Perfection

You don't have to be perfect to get better. You do need to summon the courage to trust the truth.

Shift your focus to something that makes sense. Remember: *OCD always lies.* So, when obsessions or compulsions fog my brain with confused thinking, I need to remember the logical truth. Then I have to trust the truth.

One of my refocusing techniques is to slap a statement of truth on a sticky note and then put the note on the wall. Here are a few statements that I have on my mirror in the bathroom, which is one of my more challenging places to refocus:

- Never let an OCD thought complete itself in my head.
- I will trust life a little bit more today.
- I will practice living one moment at a time.
- I will try to do the task with no interpretation.
- If a thought doesn't bring me inner peace, I don't follow it.
- That was then; this is now. I choose to stay in the present.
- Every time I challenge OCD, I weaken it.
- Every time I go into the future, I will remind myself to "get here, now."
- I choose to refocus on the truth because that's how I'll get better.

I lean on at least one of these statements every day. It helps a lot.

The next time OCD presents a "what if" question to you, try responding with "I don't know."

# Say "I Don't Know" to OCD

Like many teachers, I am good at dishing out wisdom but have to work at using that wisdom on myself. Listen, I have bad days too.

One night recently, OCD hit me hard, which triggered barrels of anxiety. But a long time ago, I was given a great tool to use against OCD, which I'd like to share with you.

The OCD thoughts mostly come in the form of a "what if" question, so I beat OCD at its own game. I repeat in my head or out loud, "I don't know" to all of OCD's "what if" questions. I don't let my mind think about any alternative answers other than, "I don't know."

OCD asks, "What if that front door isn't really locked?"

I say, "I don't know."

OCD asks, "What if you get sick and can't get well?"

I say, "I don't know."

OCD asks, "What if your loved ones get ill and it's your fault?"

I keep calm and say again, "I don't know."

Bullies ask pretty dumb questions when trying to intimidate you. But if your only response is "I don't know," you aren't playing their game. You have. to be like a stubborn mule that won't budge.

The next time OCD presents a "what if" question to you, try responding with "I don't know."

If you don't engage with the bully, you'll find some freedom.

Recovery, most of the time,
comes in pints, not gallons.

# Recovery Can Surprise You

OCD recovery can seep into your life. In my experience, it sometimes comes on fast. But most of the time it surprises you. You can do more than you think. And that goes for catching those monkey-mind obsessions too. The monkey mind is an ancient metaphor for a bunch of monkeys in your head, all giving you constant negative and catastrophizing thoughts.

In my neighborhood, we put out our garbage on Wednesday for pickup early Thursday morning. I've been practicing just taking out the garbage. You know—the "germ contamination" fear—and doing ERP therapy to push through it.

Well, the other night, I took out the garbage and, as usual, I wore plastic gloves. Not a big compromise. But my wife Jeanine doesn't wear plastic gloves, and I watched her do it with no problem. I mean, you have to trust and model someone.

So, I took out the garbage one night and realized that I didn't have my gloves on. And here's the cool part—that "seeping in" thing—I didn't care! *I did it anyway.* I guess I practiced enough and trusted enough to not care about the plastic gloves.

Now, more practice. We can get better if we trust just a little. Recovery, most of the time, comes in pints, not gallons. I'll take whatever I can get and not give up.

Always remember that you are
stronger than you think.

# Take the Risk to Do the Opposite

Take a risk today, even if it's a tiny one. You can do it. The risk to do the opposite of what OCD tells us is called "recovery." Yes, it can come with short-term discomfort. But you can handle it. Some short-term discomfort right now is worth the lasting long-term relief.

If OCD directs you to wash your hands two more times, wash your hands one more time.

If OCD moves you to think you have to go back in your car to check something, keep driving forward.

If OCD demands that you must put your spoon on the right side of your dinner plate setting, put it on the left. You get the idea.

Always remember that you are stronger than you think. Take a little risk today to do the opposite of what OCD encourages you to do. Challenge it to weaken it. Just a little. I will too.

You are doing the best you can under
the conditions you are under.

# Doing the Best You Can Is Good Enough

Most of the time, the person who is the most critical of us is ourselves. When trying to push ourselves to perfection, we create inner judgments that say we should be better and faster at recovery. This includes nonstop criticism that we aren't okay. It goes on and on.

Remember: You are doing the best you can under the conditions you are under. Give that critical mind of yours a reminder today.

One more time to get it to sink in: "I'm doing the best I can under the conditions I am under."

And that's good enough.

I do my job today for my health
and happiness tomorrow.

# It's a Part-time Job

I was complaining to my wife Jeanine today that I'm tired of having OCD for so long. I really want a huge breakthrough in research in my lifetime, preferably this year. Yet, when I notice myself getting tired, I remember that it's time to take out my acceptance hat and put it on.

I see OCD as my part-time job. (It used to be my full-time job, but treatment has helped all these years.) If I had diabetes, managing it would be my job. If I had arthritis, managing that would be my job. High blood pressure? You guessed it. Managing it would be my job. I look at OCD the same way.

None of us wants this job, that's for damn sure. But it's the job we've got, and so it's worth doing a little work daily. Why?

Jeanine—a holistic healer and teacher—says it plainly: "Healthier life, happier life."

So, I do my job today for my health and happiness tomorrow and try not to make a big deal of it. It's a job, not my identity.

You are not OCD. *You are you!* Never doubt that you deserve a happy and healthy life.

Motion is lotion for the body and brain. Get moving to feel better.

# Motion Is Lotion for the Brain

When OCD symptoms turn on and anxiety starts to rev its engine, move yourself a little. Even if you are sitting in a chair in a panic, wiggle your toes. If you can get up and walk around a bit or do light to moderate exercise, that's even better.

The more motion, the better for the brain to start to refocus and calm down the anxiety. Any movement can redirect, restart, and refocus your brain. That's working the problem.

Motion is not only lotion for your body—it's lotion for the brain. It really is.

Today, despite OCD, I choose
to be me gracefully.

# It's Okay to Just Be You

I taught college for more than 37 years, but I started to really understand teaching at about year 20. I think most teachers go through the same thing.

I learned that students wanted inspiration and mentoring over hard-core expectations. I taught in the Fine Arts department. I taught Acting for TV and Film, Television, Screenwriting, and Filmmaking. So, expectations were running high in my young students. They wanted to be film or stage stars quickly.

I remember a student who came into my office after a class in tears. He was in distress because he didn't know what he wanted to be or how to get there.

"Jim, what am I going to be?" he asked me.

I had enough years of OCD recovery and some years of mindfulness training, so I offered some advice that I had been working on myself.

Essentially, I told him, "You don't have to 'be' anything. You just have to be."

He looked at me and stopped tearing up. I think he got it.

None of us have to be anything other than ourselves at any given moment. The more genuine we are, the more accepting we are, the kinder we are, the more honest we are with ourselves and others, and the more trusting we are that we'll be okay all help to further strengthen our being-ness.

Today, despite OCD, I choose to be me gracefully.

"Do your best today to not stress over stress. Do your best today to not become fearful of the fear. Do your best today to not be anxious about the anxiety."

— Dr. Claire Weekes

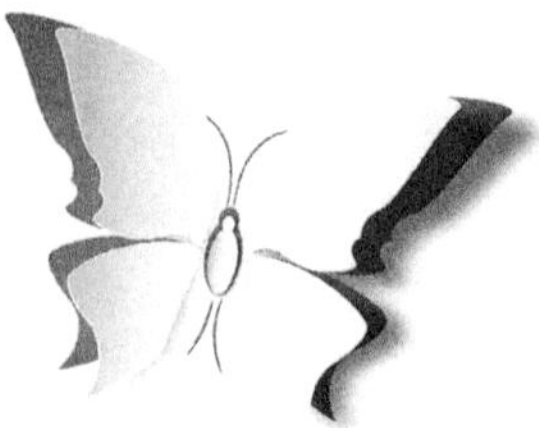

# The Anxiety Layer Cake

I learned an objective from Dr. Claire Weekes, an Australian psychiatrist and author who lived between 1903 and 1990. She had straightforward revolutionary concepts and approaches to anxiety that are still used today. The objective is simple. Not easy, but simple. Ready?

"Do your best today to not stress over stress. Do your best today to not become fearful of the fear. Do your best today to not be anxious about the anxiety."

So, you're anxious or scared or stressed. Just let those feelings be without adding another layer to them.

Repeat this to yourself: "Today, I'm going to do my best to not make an anxiety layer cake. I'll handle my anxiety one moment at a time."

Remember: You don't "have to" be perfect at any given time in your recovery.

# The Catch-Yourself Technique

After all these years with this disorder, I have become aware of how hard I am on myself when it comes to OCD. Let's face it: Life is tough enough. But life with OCD? *Please!*

What I call "The Catch-Yourself Technique" is based on awareness, self-kindness, and catching the thought and/or compulsion before it becomes full blown. OCD seems to like it when we hang on to the words "perfect" and "have to." Refocus and become aware that you don't "have to" be perfect to get better.

OCD waxes and wanes, depending on life's stress levels, and so does our recovery progress. Give yourself credit for even the smallest victory. They all count.

Can't go through a doorway? Catch yourself and know it's OCD trying to bully you. Then, just take one step toward the door, and that's good enough right now.

Have to wash your hands 25 times? Catch yourself and take the risk of washing 24 times. A small risk will always weaken OCD.

Obsessing on harm or contamination? Counter it by labeling it quickly as an OCD thought before it becomes an obsession.

We're all highly sensitive people. Today, try directing some kindness inward. Catch yourself going negative and turn it around. You can do it, and you deserve it!

Never give up hope. We just can't afford to.
Hope is too valuable. Hope disarms OCD.

# Take the Risk to Hope

Never give up hope. We just can't afford to. Hope is too valuable. Hope disarms OCD. Hope engages you in a healthy present and future. The littlest bit of hope can disrupt an anxiety attack. That means you need to take the risk to stop overly washing your hands, just a little bit for now. If you have problems like I do in the bathroom, such as taking too long on the toilet and too long in the shower, take the risk to do a little less and feel the fear or anxiety until it calms down on its own. Believe me, it will.

When you take any risk to do the opposite of what OCD urges you to do or think, you bring in hope for real recovery and change. Even if you don't fully believe in hope, fake it until you make it, and the momentum of hope will take care of the rest.

Don't ever give up on hope.

In my experience, facts create a level of certainty that can block OCD uncertainty. Even if the facts are not what I want to hear, they still bring a level of certainty and reality to my brain.

# We Have a Choice: Believe OCD or Believe Facts

OCD gives me false messages or obsessions almost daily.

"That's contaminated even though everybody else is touching it. I'm going to get sick even though there's no evidence that I will get sick."

"I'll harm others with my thoughts, even though there is no evidence that anyone can do that."

These type of obsessions feel like they could go on forever. So, what to do?

I have learned to use self-talk to calm myself down and to stick to facts the best I can. It's the art of OCD recovery to not buy into a fear and to choose to believe facts rather than OCD. Facts disarm OCD. The disorder simply cannot stand up to facts. In my experience, facts create a level of certainty that can block OCD uncertainty. Even if the facts are not what I want to hear, they still bring a level of certainty and reality to my brain.

OCD distorts reality. I would go as far as saying that OCD always lies to us. I have to catch myself all the time and choose to not go along with the distortion.

I look at the night sky and see starlight from millions of years ago. The actual star may not even be there any longer, but the light is still real. I choose to believe in the light, and I choose to believe the facts.

OCD asks me a "what if" question.
I respond with "I don't know."

# My Father's Wisdom on Decision Making

My father Jerry Callner was an extremely creative man in business and show business. He was a writer, a director, and a producer for innovative educational films for his time. He taught me filmmaking.

He was also a wise man in his quiet way. I remember him telling me about decision making. He told me that making a decision is far less anxiety-producing than not making a decision. He was not talking about the absence of thoughtfulness or contemplation but rather about simply making a decision of some kind. Even if it's a wrong decision, it's better than suffering the anxiety of agonizing and obsessing over all the possibilities.

"Obsessing": Now that's a word we all know very well. When the obsessive "what ifs" and "shoulds" and "coulds" rear their heads with a decision before me, I practice these three rules:

1. Wait, calm down, and do nothing until some decision comes.

2. If OCD riddles me with fear and "what ifs," I respond with, "I don't know."

3. If I absolutely must make a decision, I go for the most obvious choice, even if it ends up being the wrong decision.

I look at it this way: If I'm close to right, I'm in recovery. If I'm wrong, I've learned a lesson and I'm still in recovery.

My father was one wise man.

Every time you challenge OCD, you weaken it.

# Jim's 12 Daily Positive Affirmations

1. I'll take the risk to trust my senses.
2. I'll let go and stop trying to figure it out.
3. If a thought doesn't bring me inner peace, I don't follow it.
4. I'll do the task with no interpretation.
5. I'll get here, now.
6. I will stay present and remember one moment at a time.
7. I'll remember that less is more.
8. I will not allow an OCD thought to complete itself in my head.
9. I'll remember, "That was then; this is now," to keep myself centered in the present.
10. I'll do the task, and my brain will follow.
11. Every time I challenge it, I weaken it.
12. I know gratitude and appreciation will always bring me back home.

Learn to catch yourself in your mental projection room and say, "Wait a minute. This movie sucks! It's scaring me. I had better change the film."

# Change the Film Reel

When director J. J. Abrams was assigned to make the new *Star Wars* film, he brought back much of the original cast to honor the first *Star Wars* as well as he could. And he shot it in film. Not video to film, but 70 mm film. Not all movies are shot on film anymore.

This reminded me of something I learned decades ago from my great psychiatrist and mentor: "Jim, OCD creates these projections or films of fear and doubt in your mind. Your job is to recognize and become aware of that, and then change the film reel. Shift from a scary film about an imaginary future to something a bit lighter."

I never forgot that analogy. I had to change the anxious mental movie I was creating and put on a mental film reel that was something a bit more positive. You wouldn't want to see the OCD films I was creating in my mind!

I learned to catch myself in my mental projection room and say, "Wait a minute. This movie sucks! It's scaring me. I had better change the film."

So—imperfectly but with determination—I worked toward a mental movie that had a positive storyline rather than a catastrophizing one. It took a lot of attempts, but eventually this became a handy tool that I still use today.

When we do a minimal amount of recovery
work daily, we will reclaim the trust
that we are stronger than we think.

# What Do We Trust?

What do we trust? Not whom, but what? In my experience, I have come to trust that the sun will rise and set, even if it's too cloudy and we can't see it. I trust that I don't have to think about almost all the functions in my body as they just work on their own. The lungs, heart, kidneys, and liver have worked fine on their own since my birth, so I continue to trust, and do my best to take care of myself.

Though the anxiety of OCD is horrible, can I trust—like I trust my body—that the anxiety will calm down on its own, even if I do nothing? The anxiety always calms down eventually, but that's a hard idea to trust. Why don't more of us, including myself, trust that we will be okay? I believe it's about rebuilding the trust that was robbed by OCD. If we consistently do a minimal amount of recovery work daily, we will reclaim that trust and be more than okay.

The opposite of fear is trust.

# The Opposite of Fear Is Trust

How do you start reclaiming your trust today? Take a tiny baby step toward what you fear daily.

After all these years of struggling with fears, I have come firmly to this conclusion: *The opposite of fear is trust.*

Here's the in-your-face truth: OCD is about fear, and trust is about peace. OCD doesn't hold up in the presence of real trust. My goal is to fight life less and trust life more. It's a minute-by-minute choice to trust, but it can create a lifetime of serenity and calm.

Thoughts are not actions, and thoughts are not facts. Thoughts come and go. They are nothing else.

# What If vs. What Is

Obsessions—or, as I call them, "what ifs." If you think your "what ifs" are special only to you, think again. I've been around people with OCD for more than 38 years, and nothing so far has knocked me off my seat. It's all fear, including my own.

Remember: It's all under the category of doubt, which creates fear, which creates anxiety, which creates more "what ifs." Pretty bleak, huh? So, what is the antidote to the "what ifs"?

When a "what if" sneaks into my consciousness, I become aware of it and turn my fearful "what if" into the fact-based "what is."

"What is" means putting your attention on facts. Is it a fact that washing your hands 40 to 50 times or more is needed to keep germs away? No. Why? The fact is that your hands have layers of skin and oils that protect you and everyone else.

Is once or twice good enough? Yes. That's a common and true fact.

Does having any obsession mean that you are going to do something bad or have done something bad? Nope.

Thoughts are not actions, and thoughts are not facts. Thoughts come and go. They are nothing else.

I take the power out of any OCD obsession by turning to these "what is" facts. It helps calm me down. It's a great way to practice recovery.

Today, if the false "what if" is jerking you around, notice it gracefully and patiently, and then shift to "what is."

Show your brain that there is no danger,
and your brain will eventually follow.
It will always follow. You just have to
take the initial risk and practice.

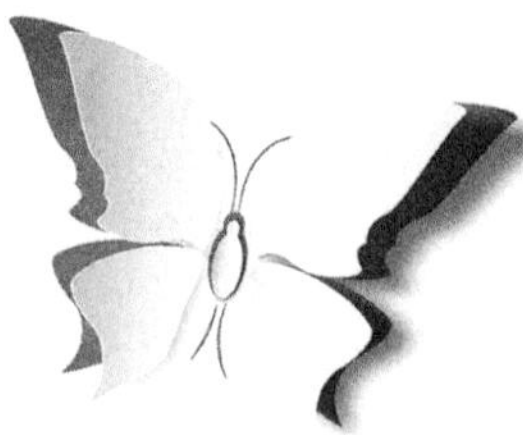

# Take the Risk and the Brain Will Follow

I remember getting out of the hospital in 1983 after a six-week stay for severe OCD. My psychiatrist was quite brilliant. (He stuck with me for the next 28 years.) He gave me the assignment to get out of the house and walk around the mall. He wanted me to practice being among people. Even if I didn't communicate with them, I would be among them and see that nothing bad would happen.

So, off to the mall I went for my daily walks. I simply circled the indoor mall a few times. At first, it was tough even though it was not an overwhelming amount of people. But, of course, like all exposure, it got easier in time. It was so important to my recovery process. I had to show my brain that there was no danger, and my brain eventually followed. It will always follow. You just have to take the initial risk and practice.

To this day, I sometimes force myself to get out of the house. Why? It's all part of the management of the recovery process. We are born to be social. Being around or with people is recovery. Practice taking the risk and the brain will follow.

At your core, you are not OCD. You are a kind, a loving, an imaginative, a creative, a super sensitive, an empathic, and a heartfelt being.

# You Are Not OCD. You Are You.

Many of us with OCD think we are bad people if we have bad thoughts. I'm here to tell you that this just isn't true. Simply because OCD can create thoughts and obsessions that are horrible to think about doesn't mean that those thoughts are you. The thoughts might be bad, but remember that you aren't bad because of the thoughts.

This is the nature of the disorder. It attacks your morals and values. You get trapped into believing the OCD thought and suddenly you think you are a bad person. When I get these thoughts, it's my challenge to ignore them, label them as OCD, and move on. I remember that it's OCD, not me. Thoughts are not facts or actions. They are just thoughts. You and I are not OCD thoughts.

So, who are we? At our core, we are kind, loving, imaginative, creative, super sensitive, empathic, heartfelt beings. The next time those OCD thoughts creep in and try to convince you that you are bad, smile, label them as OCD, and remember who you *really* are at your core.

You are not OCD. You are you.

Every time OCD reminds me of what I seemingly can't do, I remind myself of what I can do and what I have done.

# What I Can Do

I think many of us are conditioned through life to focus on what we can't do rather than focus on what we can do and what we have done.

When I was in the hospital years ago with severe OCD, my psychiatrist said something very important to me that I would come to understand more deeply later: "The patient is the last one to see progress."

I don't know about you, but I tend to get so enmeshed in the problem that I miss the strides I have taken forward—even the tiny ones.

Currently, I'm trying my best to practice a process of self-reminding. Every time OCD reminds me of what I seemingly can't do, I remind myself what I can do and what I have done.

Most of the time I say it out loud so I can hear myself. The internal dialogue usually goes like this:

OCD: "You can't get out of the shower in less than 15 minutes."

Me: "Wait a minute! I can and have gotten out of my shower rituals in less than 10 minutes. I've done it several times and can and want to do it again. I can and I will!"

So, the next time you think, "I can't," remind yourself that "I want to, and I can." Even if you are not ready to believe it, you're planting the seeds of recovery. Saying it sends the right signals to your subconscious. You can do much more than you think.

When you do the opposite of what
OCD demands, you are rewiring
your brain for the good.

# Self-Talk

Why is it important to have some kind of dialog with yourself when you are struggling with OCD symptoms? Well, before I answer that question from my own perspective, let me ask you a question.

Have you ever had a positive or nurturing obsession and/or compulsion caused by OCD? My answer is "never." Obsessions that have led me to compulsions have always been negative in some way. In my experience with recovery, self-talk counters the negativity that OCD delivers. Even if you don't fully believe the words you are saying to yourself, your subconscious will still follow your lead.

Here are some examples:

OCD says, "You are going to panic right now."

You counter with self-talk: "I've been here before, and I handled it. If you bat me around, I will actually get stronger."

OCD says, "You may harm someone with that thought."

You counter with self-talk: "Nice try, OCD, but that's not who I am. I have higher values than your bizarre obsessions."

OCD says, "You have to wash your hands or you will be contaminated."

You counter with self-talk: "I don't have to do anything you say because I'm in control here ... not you!"

When OCD nags me with negativity or challenges, my own self-talk always leads me to these words: "Yeah, yeah, yeah ... heard it before, but I ain't going down that road today."

Now you tell me which feels like recovery: countering OCD with positive self-talk or buying into OCD horror stories?

I choose positive self-talk every time.

I've come to two bottom-line questions for OCD recovery that I ask myself almost every day. I answer "yes" to both.

1. Am I willing to trust?
2. Am I willing to take the risk to challenge OCD?

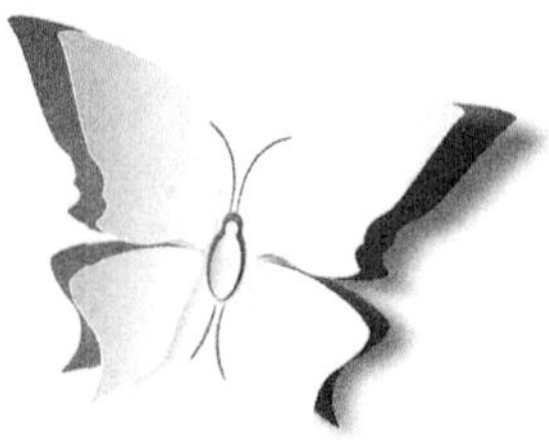

# Trust and Risk

The last 38 years: hospitalization, living alone in an apartment using plastic plates and utensils, long nights of anxiety, hours and hours of hand-washing, checking rituals, obsessions, CBT, ERP therapy, teaching college in spite of OCD, 12-Step programs, relationships, getting married, being bullied, making movies on OCD, relapsing, and many ups and downs.

One word sums up my continuing recovery: trust.

First, whom am I trusting? The people who have taught me that there's no danger. Therapists, friends, family members—anyone intuitively I can trust.

Second, how do I risk? Well, I use trust as an anchor and go for it. No way around that. You need to go for it and trust to rewire the brain.

Guess what? You do get better. I'm not completely cured, but I'll take "in the process of getting better" any time.

Trust, risk, and work toward recovery. It truly pays off.

The ones who love us despite OCD are
the angels who walk among us.

# Love Equals Acceptance

What does love mean? Is it a feeling? Is it something indescribable?

In a college class I taught called "The Confidence Class," we talked about love a lot. I described it to my young students like this: "Love equals acceptance. Love is acceptance." It's a lot more, of course, but I still believe that acceptance is at the core of love.

So, now you are struggling with OCD and anxiety. You want to be loved by family and friends, but not everyone accepts your illness. They are afraid to. They feel powerless. What to do?

I was taught to find "like-people"—those who would accept or love me unconditionally, like an extended family. Convincing, explaining, and trying so hard to be accepted and loved by anyone in spite of OCD seem virtually impossible. However, being among like-people who already "get it" gives you a compassionate, accepting, loving common bond whether or not you know them personally.

I've been in real-life and private Internet OCD support groups for years—especially Facebook, where you can find many of them. It has always been the "go-to" place to find acceptance when stigma or ignorance would cloud love in others. I learned a tough lesson early on: You can't control how someone thinks, acts, or behaves. You can't force someone to love you if they don't want to. But love is acceptance.

The ones who love us despite OCD are the angels who walk among us.

Can we get better? With just a little willingness and courage, yes. We absolutely can.

# Can We Get Better? (Part 1)

Sometimes people ask me if they can truly get better. I asked myself that same question in 2009 when I had a relapse after my mother passed just two months from her 90th birthday.

I had been managing OCD fairly well with the usual ups and downs for years and years, but this loss hit me extremely hard. Grief is sloppy and tough to feel, and it's my belief that we will often cling to anything else to not feel it. As dysfunctional and painful as OCD is on the body and mind, it was still more familiar to me than grief. So, I relapsed. But I knew that I had to continue my teaching job at the college.

As Billy Joel once said about his touring at age 65, "I have to occupy my mind, or my mind will occupy me."

I had to keep teaching to keep my mind occupied in a healthy way before my mind came up with far less healthy ways of occupying itself.

Two of my OCD rituals had gone through the roof: showering and checking. We live on a huge hill above the ocean in Aptos, California. My wife Jeanine would coach me with ERP therapy for the shower, but my orders for the checking came from my therapist.

"It takes courage to not be discouraged."
— Ben Ferencz

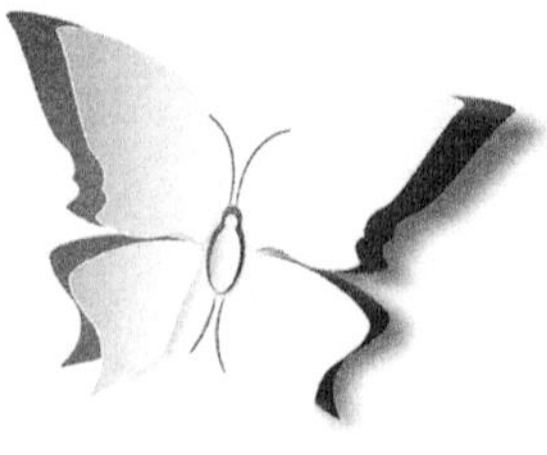

# Can We Get Better? (Part 2)

What was I checking for? At the time, I was mostly afraid of stepping in something that my obsessional mind told me would eventually harm someone via contamination. It was untrue, of course, but I was convinced in my season of grief.

My therapist told me to walk up and down that hill every night and not turn around or look back to check. I knew I had to get better to keep working, so for one summer I took on that hill every night with a flashlight in my hand. The stars above were beautiful, but my eyes were trying not to look down and "check."

The first month was constant, relentless checking. I was okay going down, but every few feet I'd stop on the way up, sweating profusely, and then retrace my steps. In the second month, I challenged myself more, refusing to look back. By the third month, I was walking up that hill without much checking at all.

Was it hard? *Oh, yes!*

Was it frustrating? *Incredibly.*

Did it eventually work? *It really, truly did.*

Now, on days when stress hits, I may look back and "check" for 5 seconds or so, but I always remember the ERP therapy I did on the hill during those summer nights. It is now my mental anchor, which I can take with me through any emotional season.

Can we get better? With just a little willingness and courage, yes. We absolutely can. As Ben Ferencz (the famous and now 100-year-old American lawyer and prosecutor in World War II) said, "It takes courage to not be discouraged."

The small steps toward recovery count too.
They will add up quickly with practice.

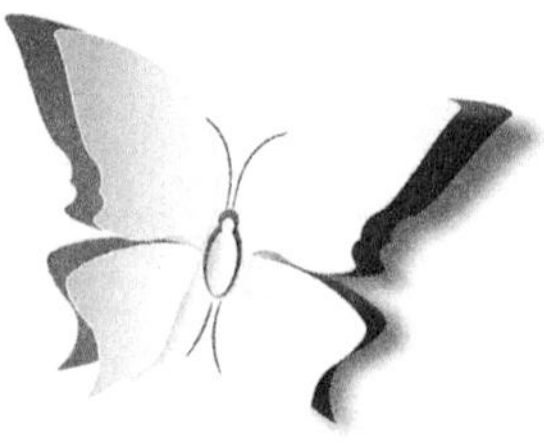

# One Step

"The journey of 1000 miles begins with one step."

— *Tao Te Ching*, by Lao Tzu, ancient Chinese philosopher

*Tao Te Ching* has been known to mean "The Book of the Way and its Virtue." People believe the book was written around 600 BC.

I have learned much from this simple yet complex ancient book. But this particular teaching of taking one step at a time helps me daily.

Take just one step toward recovery today. You can take another step tomorrow.

Believe me ... it will gain momentum.

Complaining begets more complaining and positive begets more positive. Your choice.

# Complaining Begets Complaining

While I write this post, I'm wearing a reminder T-shirt that I got some years ago with this title on it: "No Complaining."

I have a black belt in complaining. I grew up in a family and culture that complained as a way to communicate and gossip. When I was in my 50s, I was taught that whatever we put out there, we get more of. Complaining begets more complaining. And, if you have OCD like me, it latches on to whatever you feed it.

But it's a balance. I used to teach my students that "the suppression of expression" is what really screws you up. We of course need to express our feelings whether they are good, bad, confused, fearful, or critical.

But here's the deal: It's the amount that counts. More complaining brings you not only more complaining but more fears and symptoms. So, I always remain aware of the amount of *kvetching* (Yiddish for "complaining") I do with others and to myself. Some amount of expressing your frustrations might help you get something off your chest, but the vast majority of complaining is just not useful.

I'm only interested in solutions and soothing, whether it comes internally or externally.

Facing any fear is a solution.

Mindfulness is a solution.

Refocusing is a solution.

Gracefulness is a solution.

Helping someone else, even if you are struggling yourself, is a solution.

So, that's my rant ... at least I wasn't complaining.

Lightness and laughter are some
of the best healing medicines.

# Can We Laugh at OCD?

I was thinking that OCD is serious business. The disorder itself is very serious, and moving through daily recovery is serious stuff too. But can we learn to take ourselves not so seriously? Can we laugh?

My experience is that you never laugh "at someone" with a disability ... ever! It's just plain cruel. Whether it's diabetes or OCD or whatever, you just don't.

Can you laugh "with someone" who is suffering? Yes, if it's appropriate in the moment. You can also cry.

Over several decades, I've used a technique to shift the anxiety and panic energy with the folks I help. I've received calls or messages in the middle of the night from someone in a panic. I respectfully listen and let them talk it out for a while because I almost always have been there myself.

But then I ask a simple question: "What did you have for dinner?"

Usually, this kind of question shocks the person, but they meekly say something like pasta or soup.

I ask, "What kind of pasta and soup?"

Then, I hear the shift: a change of tone in their voice. They are coming back to this moment, and eventually we are laughing together, which helps everything.

It doesn't happen all the time, but is lightness and laughter healing? You know the answer.

I'm not in the future. I'm not in the past.
I'm simply in the present, doing the task.

# Anxiety Lives in the Future

I teach what I need to learn. So, if I'm stuck washing or checking or having any compulsion or obsession, I remind myself what I remind you: *Be present.* I know that OCD is keeping me stuck and that I have to bring myself back to the present moment.

If I'm having an obsession, I name it "OCD thinking" to tame it and do my best to move on.

If I get stuck in any ritual, I take the risk to slow down and stop, even if it causes anxiety, since I know that anxiety will never last if I am patient and sit with it.

Anxiety lives in a magical future that hasn't happened yet; in most cases, these imagined futures won't happen. Fixating on these unreal futures creates fear. OCD can live in the past too in the form of regret or fear of something that has happened.

But when you get into the present, OCD doesn't have a chance. It truly has nothing to counter when you practice mindfulness.

As my wife Jeanine says, "Get here, now," which means get in the present and do what is in front of you for your own higher good.

So, here's my little teaching for today, and it comes in the form of a powerful mantra: "I'm not in the future. I'm not in the past. I'm simply in the present, doing the task."

The more you remind yourself of staying present and mindful, the more it becomes a powerful healing tool.

Comforting words matter.

# The Serenity Prayer for Anxiety

Some years back, I had a surgery to remove a mole on my forehead. It went well, but we all know how fear and anxiety can completely take over our thinking. Leading up to this necessary surgery, I was really trying to hold it together. I had some bad nights, but I got through it.

I'm not a very religious man, and I know that the "G" word does set some people off, so take what you want from this message and leave the rest.

I've used the below prayer for decades to refocus, calm down, re-center, and come back to the present moment. You don't have to believe in anything for it to work; the words are wise and comforting in themselves.

Many of you have heard of the Serenity Prayer. I was told to gently repeat it to myself until my anxiety slowed down, and it works well for me. It's worth a try.

*God, grant me the serenity*
*to accept the things I cannot change,*
*the courage to change the things I can,*
*and the wisdom to know the difference.*

I choose life, with all its uncertainty, all its choices, and all its risks. I choose to be strong and get better.

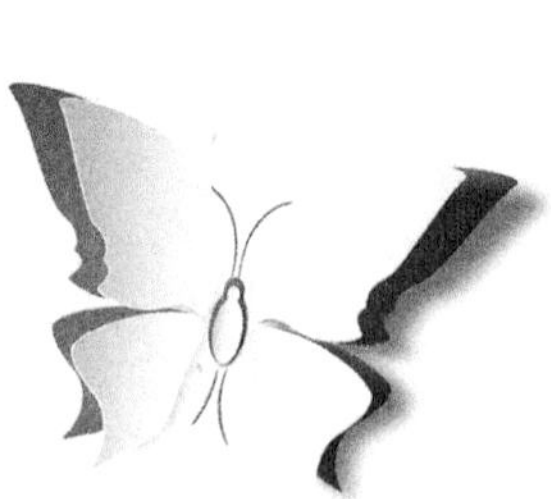

# Living with Uncertainty and Doing the Opposite of What OCD Demands

So, here's the deal: OCD demands that you doubt, right? It demands that you always have certainty and safety. Life, however, inherently offers uncertainty and risk-taking.

As my ancestors would say, "*Oy vey!*"

What to do? Instead of demanding impossible certainty, I choose life, with all its uncertainty, all its choices, and all its risks.

There are some things that most of us can be certain about:

- You can be certain that the sun will rise, even if you can't see it through the storm.
- You can be certain that you love your children.
- You can be certain that you love your friends and the special relationships in your life.
- I'm certain that I love my wife Jeanine and vice versa.
- I'm certain enough to enjoy my life.
- I believe we can be certain that we are stronger than we think.

The challenge is to live with uncertainty, even if we are uncomfortable with it. Learning to go through life with uncertainty puts us on the track to better understanding that it will all work out, no matter what. By the way, if things don't work out, you'll handle it. That's how life works—according to me anyway.

OCD doesn't like acceptance. It thrives on doubt.

Forget about doubt. Doubt is such a waste of energy, and our energy is not infinite.

Practice doing the opposite of what OCD demands, one step at a time. This takes the power out of OCD every time. That I know for certain.

We just can't afford the luxury
of negative thinking.

# Negative Thinking Is an Expensive Luxury

I was listening to some of my favorite people: Dr. Wayne Dyer and Esther and Abraham Hicks. I've been following them for years, and these people have great wisdom and teachings on how to live life.

I heard something that struck me big time from Esther and Abraham: "If we were more unwilling to put up with negative emotions, our lives would become much easier."

I get so caught up with negativity toward myself and life that it's really tiring and depleting. Aren't we all tired of being tired? Part of it has to do with all the negative emotions we're fed and the emotions we create.

It helps to counter negative, scary emotions with thoughts that are even a little more positive. An unwillingness to put up with negative emotions is a recovery state of being. I'm never perfect at anything, but I'm having a go at this lately, and it does shift my negative feelings. Even if the only positive thought I can create is that we are having pasta for dinner tonight, that's good enough for the shift.

By the way, if you're unsure of how or what to replace the negative emotions with, try gratitude or appreciation. Being grateful and appreciating nature, music, or a friend are good ways to start. *We just can't afford the luxury of negative thinking.*

Let's spend our precious time on things that give us more positive returns.

Breathe slowly, reset, refocus.

# Take a Time-out from the OCD Conversation

Sometimes you just have to take a time-out from the OCD conversation and move on. Know what I mean? For example, you're standing in front of a locked door, staring at the lock. It looks locked, but your brain is screaming at you that it's not locked.

Then, the dysfunctional OCD conversation begins in your brain: "It's locked, but what if it's not locked enough? No, it's locked. I can see that it's locked. But what if someone can get in? No, they can't. It's a locked door!"

This scenario can go on for hours in some cases. You could pick any compulsion or obsession, and it's basically the same mental argument.

Instead, I choose to time-out of this circular conversation in my head and move on. Yes, it takes courage and can be riddled with anxiety at any level. But, when I take the lead—by putting my mental foot down, refusing to participate in the conversation, walking away for a few minutes, breathing slowly, resetting, and refocusing—I know I'm getting better.

We can all do it. We can time-out of the OCD conversation for just a moment to realign with what's real and factual.

Feeling good is fundamentally
about a shift in attitude.

# Having It All and Still Feeling Horrible

My wife Jeanine and I live on the Monterey Bay, and we take walks by the ocean every day. It's a beautiful place to live.

I was talking to a friend who also has OCD, and we chatted about the big question: "How can we live in such a beautiful place, have pretty much everything we need, and still feel so horrible?"

Well, the trap right there is equating the place with how you should feel. I found out the hard way, like most of you, that healing is an inside job.

Don't get me wrong. I love where we live and what we have. But feeling good is fundamentally about a shift in attitude, calming the mind through practice, breathing slowly, appreciating everything, and—most importantly, no matter where you live—staying present.

Monitor your inner dialogue. Recognize and identify what sounds and feels like an OCD thought. Label it as an OCD bully playing with you again—but refuse to play.

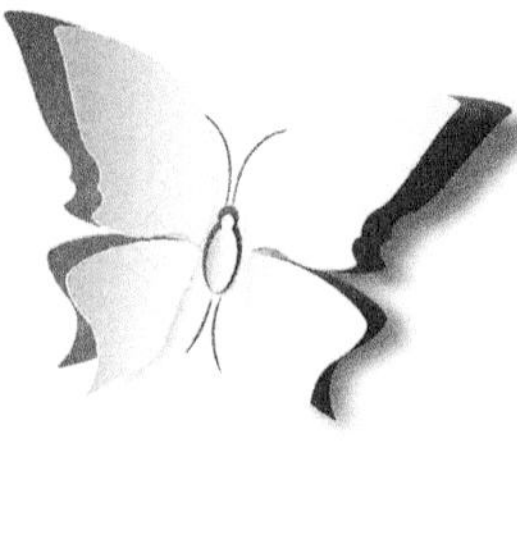

# The OCD Recovery Trick That Works

So, here's the deal: I define my OCD symptoms as a "twitchy amygdala": the fight-or-flight or startle response that can go off at any time and with any stress. The trick I have found and practice is to monitor or become aware of that response and not fight it.

What do I do? I become aware that it's OCD and not a threat. For me, 99.9999% the time, it's OCD bullying me. I'm not kidding. I practice dismissing the thought as a bully (even though it will return and be persistent).

I still persist right back, and I slow down my breathing. If appropriate, I may need medication or to talk to someone for a reality check—not reassurance but a voice of reason or an empathic voice.

I've been practicing the dismissal part for some years now, and I've gotten better at it. Just know that it is achievable. Trust that you are going to be okay at any given moment if you put in the minimum amount of awareness. *Really.*

Develop an attitude of gratitude and appreciation. It will help everything heal.

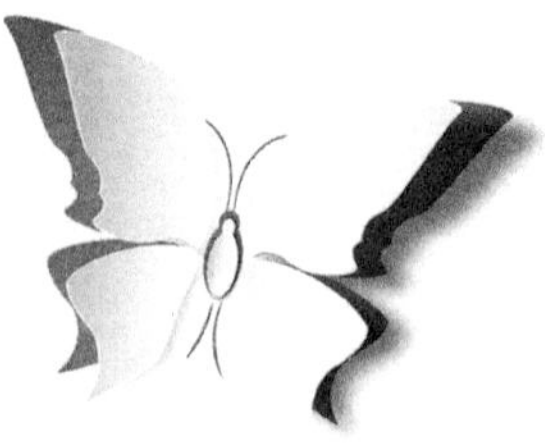

# The Power of Appreciation and Gratitude

I usually don't pick up our mail as my wife Jeanine gets to it before I do. But this day was my turn, and I went out to our mailbox across the street. I've had trouble with that box. The box isn't really the problem; it's more about the "checking ritual" at the box.

You all know what I mean: those old OCD "what ifs":

"What if there are bad germs on the box and I bring them back into the house?"

"What if I touch those germs, and then touch Jeanine and she becomes sick?"

All irrational and OCD thinking as usual. But, this time, I just opened the box, took out the mail, and walked back toward the house. No checking at all.

As I was walking back, I became aware that I didn't check or even want to check. It was disarming.

I asked myself, "Is this what it feels like to be free?"

It really felt good! Why, on this day of all other days, didn't I check? Well, I noticed it was a day in which I was feeling appreciative and grateful for my life, even with OCD.

Does noticing how we feel and working on appreciation and gratitude make a difference in stopping rituals? Sounds too simple and good to be true, right? The fact is that it really can make all the difference.

Don't forget that laughter heals
too. It's okay to laugh.

# Occupy Your Mind Before Your Mind Occupies You

I think a lot of us have an unconscious tendency to get down, and it takes a conscious effort for us to keep ourselves balanced emotionally and mentally. It doesn't necessarily have to be a big action to shift out of those feelings. Almost any kind of forward movement helps.

I go out on walks to take photos. Photography takes my fearful thinking and focuses it onto something outside of myself, which is beautiful. Research shows that beauty can shift the "downs" to the "middles," and I'll take the "middle" feelings any time.

So, I drag myself into the car and take the three-minute trip to the ocean. My mind likes to take over if I'm not careful, so I choose to search for any visual stimulus that helps me refocus. For me, it usually takes the form of ocean and landscape photography.

There are endless ways to shift the "down" feelings into "middle" feelings: music, a simple breathing meditation, talking to a friend, positive movies or television shows, and any laughter.

Choose something to occupy your mind before your mind occupies you.

Acceptance is a big part of recovery. The more you resist, the more it persists. Be willing to be vulnerable.

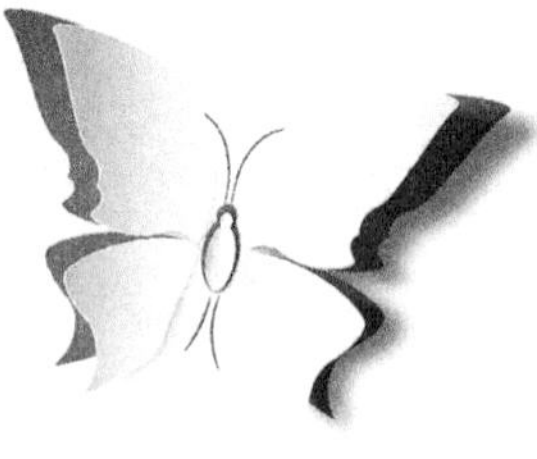

# OCD Always Lies

Well, does OCD always lie? It's safe enough to say that OCD always lies because the percentage of truth within an OCD thought is so low.

I asked a well-known OCD therapist and director of The OCD Treatment Centre in England this exact question: "Can I say to myself and to others whom I help that OCD always lies?"

She replied, "Absolutely, because the outrageous thoughts just don't hold up to reality enough."

Is there any amount of truth to an OCD thought? I have to say, in some cases, yes. But there is also some truth in the thought that a meteor the exact size of your house will land on your house tonight. Get my drift?

In my experience, I need to acknowledge and accept that there may be some truth to some OCD thoughts and that acceptance is part of recovery too. But it's so minuscule that I can hold onto the anchor that OCD always lies. You can too.

Think of OCD as a four-year-old bully who never grows up. Never trust bullies.

# Interrupting Thoughts Before They Become Beliefs

A belief emerges from something you think repeatedly. OCD obsessions fit nicely in this definition. Great. Now what? Well, a belief may be something you think over and over, but no one ever said a belief is forever or that you can't question a thought.

Here's an example of interrupting thoughts before they become beliefs: I'm taking a walk and suddenly get the thought that "I have to" go back and retrace my steps.

Now, here's where the work and choices come into play: Before I start ruminating on "I have to go back and check," I question the thought: "Is this OCD at work, or is there really a logical reason to go back and check?"

If you label a thought as OCD, there is never a reason to go back. Why? Because OCD always lies, remember? So, now that I've interrupted the thought before it repeats and becomes a belief, I drum up the courage to trust myself and move on.

Is this easy? Of course not. But it does get easier in time, and it's far better than believing in lies that keep you comfortable but stagnant in your recovery.

Slowing down the momentum of OCD fears with mindfulness is one of the most powerful tools to get better.

# Momentum of the Mind

I came up with an idea that I call the "momentum of the mind." First, something triggers our fear, and then our narratives kick in. The story starts to pick up speed and momentum the more we think about it. More layers of fear pile on top of an already scary story.

Then, as you know, the anxiety accompanies the narrative you've been telling yourself, which causes a whirlwind of mental catastrophes.

So, how do you slow down the momentum of the mind? The reason mindfulness is such a big deal for us is that it's about awareness. I prefer to call it "mindful awareness." You see, the practice of simply becoming aware that your mind is taking off with an OCD story slows it down. I know it sounds too easy, and you're right. In reality, this takes a lot of practice. The good news is that you don't have to be perfect at it to reap its benefits.

When I get scared—usually about my health—and OCD triggers the scary scenarios in my mind that are simply not true, I kick in the mindful awareness.

"Oh, wait a minute," I say. "All this awfulness is OCD again, and OCD always lies."

Just saying these words to myself helps me become aware that the story isn't me ... it's OCD. Slowing down the momentum with mindfulness or mindful awareness is one of the most powerful tools to get better.

Understand that surrendering does not mean giving up. Surrendering is a means of handling anxiety and panic that accompanies OCD.

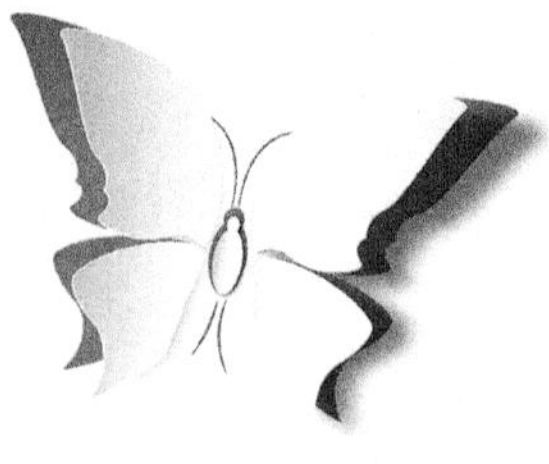

# Surrendering Is Part of the Fight

I had a brilliant psychiatrist for more than 27 years. He retired at age 75, but we still keep in touch. He was and is a very spiritual man—not necessarily religious but spiritually minded—and he taught me how to reclaim my spirit by letting go. He taught me about the real meaning of the word "surrender." It didn't mean submitting to OCD and just letting it ruin your life; rather, surrendering is a means of handling anxiety and panic that accompanies OCD.

In early therapy, surrendering sounded like I was giving up. After some time, I realized it meant just the opposite. My psychiatrist was teaching me to feel the feelings until they dissipated on their own.

To this day, I still respond to OCD anxiety with, "Yeah, yeah. Go ahead and bat me around. I surrender. I've been here before and know that when I fight my emotions rather than feel them, you just bring on more. So, have at it. I am not playing your game."

Do I use other approaches of calming down, like refocusing my thoughts, breathing, exercise, and meditation? Yes.

When my mother passed in 2006, I called this psychiatrist in anxiety and grief and asked, "How am I going to handle this?"

He gave me the same response I first heard from him nearly 30 years before: "Feel the feelings, Jim."

We talk about fighting so often, but I know that surrendering is a way to fight and get longer lasting results.

Accepting that OCD pulls us in and out of the forest is part of getting better.

# Walking Out of the Woods

When people ask me how I am doing after all these years, my answer usually goes like this: "Well, I'm out of the woods but not quite out of the forest!"

Accepting that OCD pulls us in and out of the forest is part of getting better. Hey, I may be in the forest for the rest of my life, but it's better than hanging around those deep, dark woods.

How do we walk out of the woods? I was told long ago at the beginning of this whole thing that you simply put one foot in front of the other and take a step. One step at a time. Every time I find myself running from fear and impatience rather than gracefully stepping away, I start getting anxious and feel like I'm back in the woods.

So, don't run. Just focus on slowing down and taking one step at a time, and then slowly, mindfully, you'll be walking out of the woods too.

Make your highest good to get better—one step at a time.

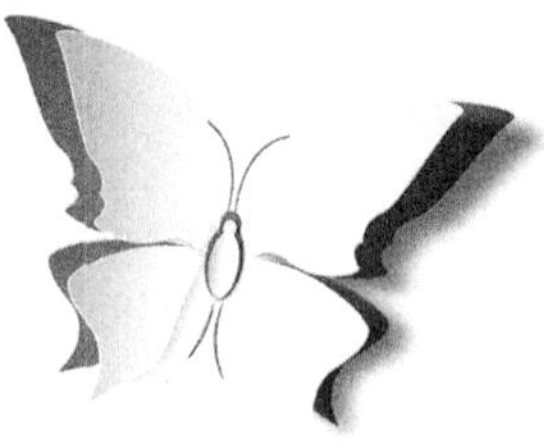

# Your Highest Good

Sometimes you've just got to push through and do it for the highest good—whatever "highest good" means to you. For me, my highest good is my health, my relationships, my friends, my wife, and my life. I keep my sights on my personal highest good, and it helps to keep me moving forward.

Find your highest good, and let it move you forward today.

Fact: OCD is a neurobiological disorder.
Stigma: We all have a little OCD.

# The Stigma: "I Think Everyone Has a Little OCD"

I met a stylist at the salon where I get my hair cut. (Yes, even when you have very little hair like I do, you still need to get haircuts.)

Thinking I made feature films, she expressed interest in my work and asked, "So what kind of movies have you made?"

"Probably nothing you have seen," I responded. "I make movies about recovery from OCD."

She smiled. "Oh, *really*?" Then came the phrase we all have heard too often: "I think we all have a little OCD!"

I know ... cringe city. But it was also a chance to educate someone about that stigma one more time.

I replied nicely, "No, not everyone does. That's the stigma aboumantrat OCD that a lot of people don't understand."

She replied, "Well, I think I have some OCD."

I asked her a question that almost always stops folks in their tracks: "When you obsess about something or have a compulsion, do you get intense anxiety?"

"Well, no," she said after a few quiet moments.

"That's the main difference between the stigmatized version of OCD and someone with real, clinical OCD. OCD is accompanied by sometimes disabling anxiety and panic."

"Really?"

"Yes," I answered and gave her my website with my OCD coaching videos.

You can't educate them all, but maybe now that stylist will think twice before promoting a stigma. Oh ... I still got a good haircut!

Find your break in the darkness, pay attention to any little bits of light, and learn to focus on the light you have rather than the darkness that has you.

# Find Light through Darkness

Don't underestimate the light. Just when I feel like I'm falling apart and can't handle it, light always comes through.

There were times where the light was a slogan that reminded me that I was going to be okay, or it was helping someone who was in a much worse situation than I was. In years past, going to a movie redirected my attention and gave me something to refocus on. Now, daily, the light is taking a walk in nature, which helps reorient my fearful thoughts into peaceful thoughts.

Sometimes I don't see any light because I'm so engulfed and so identified with the anxious thinking. But, even if I do nothing, it does pass. It will eventually calm down, even if only by a small amount. Sometimes just a small amount is the best you can do in the moment. Believe me, after more than 38 years of this mental illness, I have sharpened my ability to notice any glimmer of light that shines through the darkness.

My wife Jeanine and I take walks by the ocean almost every day. It's a sacred connection time for us. We walk, and I take pictures. Our walks remind me that there is always some light through the thoughts, anxiety, panic, and darkness.

Find your break in the darkness, pay attention to any little bits of light, and learn to focus on the light you have rather than the darkness that has you.

When my OCD thoughts take off into the future and make me scared and foggy, I say to myself, "Come back." I do it until I calm down into the present. It works.

# Come Back

One of the best tools I have found for obsessions and/or compulsions that lead to panic and anxiety and catastrophizing about the future is the repetition of two powerful words: "Come back."

In my experience with almost any form of stress, my mind will take off into the future, and the scary and negative OCD scenarios will start. My head is foggy, and I have a feeling that I'm not here or present.

But words have immense power to bring you back to clarity. As many times as I need to, and until I feel a shift, I say to myself, "Come back, Jim." I am asking myself to come back to the present, come back to doing or focusing on what's in front of me, and especially come back to gratitude.

When you come back to being grateful for the littlest things, anxiety cannot compete. It cannot coexist when you are in a state of gratitude. So, right now, *come back.*

Anxiety will pass even if you just wait it out. If you catch your breathing and slowly bring it down—it will pass sooner.

# Wait It Out

When anxiety hits, sometimes the best thing to do is simply wait it out. Yes, refocusing helps, breathing really helps, talking it out helps, medication helps, and meditation can help.

Mostly, know deep down that it will pass if you don't fight it. It's a powerful "knowing" that you can keep in the back pocket of your mind.

Believe me, you'll get through it—just like I do and like many others like us do every day.

Say to yourself, "I have no room for lies right now," which will help a lot in taking your power back.

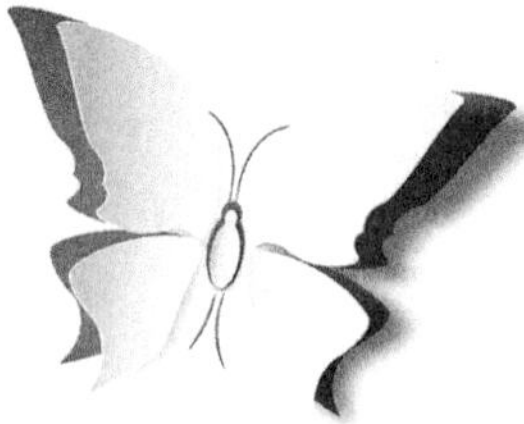

# Do What's in Front of You to Stay Present

I used to teach filmmaking. I always taught my college students that basic cinematic and photographic composition is based on foreground, middle ground, and background.

As a photographer, I have to know how to properly frame the subjects of my compositions. If there were too many trees or too many clouds, it wouldn't be as strong of a picture. You must stay focused on your subject, not letting the background or foreground overwhelm. Do you see where I'm going with this metaphor?

I've been having a lot of background OCD chatter lately. The noise of worry takes up the background of my thoughts. I work hard at staying focused, but that chatter is always there. For me, reframing my thoughts and goals as I would frame a photograph helps me focus on the bigger picture. The chatter may go on in the background, but remaining mindful of my goals and staying in the present help me stay balanced.

If you are living with OCD, try reframing the picture when your thoughts start crowding in.

Say to yourself, "I have no room for lies right now," which will help a lot in taking your power back.

Reframe your thoughts mindfully and in the present moment, which is all we have anyway.

Hope begets hope, acceptance begets acceptance, and any small step I take forward begets bigger steps. It's called the "Law of Attraction in Action."

# Law of Attraction in Action

How many times in my life have I said the words, "I hate OCD"? In more than 38 years of living with OCD, it's probably reached into the thousands. We all have these thoughts from time to time. How could we *not* come to hate OCD?

But here's the catch: It does no good to "hate" because OCD matches your negative emotions and feeds off them. If I keep ranting or banging the drum of how much I hate it, what do I get? I only amplify my thoughts and emotions of hatred for OCD.

On the other hand, when I work toward accepting and doing something about my struggles with OCD—even in the smallest way—I start to recover with hope. Hope beats out hate. Always.

So, I have to catch myself when I want to hate and instead remember to take action on what I *do* want. Hope begets hope, acceptance begets acceptance, and any small step I take forward begets bigger steps. It's called the "Law of Attraction in Action."

I choose change for my higher good.

# I Choose Change for My Higher Good

Nothing changes if nothing changes. Change is hard. Change takes standing up to OCD for your higher good. But what we must realize is that change oftentimes comes about slowly. It sure has for me. I challenge OCD, but it's not a straight line upward.

The line on the graph of recovery generally trends upward, but there are also plenty of rises and falls. I fall, get back up, calm down, and try again. When I accept the fact that at least I'm working toward change and put less focus on my setbacks, I feel better. At least I'm doing something! And that is infinitely better than worrying and doing nothing.

Bit by bit, behavior by behavior, thought by thought, I choose change over fear for the sake of my higher good.

Use this mantra even if you don't fully believe it yet, and your subconscious will eventually get it: "I choose change for my higher good."

Be graceful with yourself
today. You deserve it.

# The Power of Being Graceful in Recovery

My wife Jeanine and I like to go down to the famous Monterey Bay Aquarium and watch the jellyfish. They are a wonder of nature. As I watch these beautiful animals take their poised time as they move around their environments, I am reminded that I must take recovery gracefully.

In my experience, OCD triggers the "oh, no!" and "hurry up!" thoughts. Obviously, giving in to that way of fearful thinking just gets me more anxious, and then it becomes a frantic cycle.

As soon as I encounter those triggering thoughts, I have trained myself to say directly, "No, I'm going to slow down and take it gracefully this time. One step at a time. I will just do what's in front of me with as much mindful focus as I can. I will choose to not give into the OCD thinking, and I'm going to do the task gracefully."

Guess what happens? I begin to feel empowered, and the anxiety starts to calm down. Whether it's washing too much, showering too much, or overthinking a fear, I choose to be graceful in my recovery.

We all can learn something from the jellyfish: Be graceful with yourself today.

Thoughts are not facts,
they are just thoughts.

# Taking a Shower

Many of us have problems taking a shower. I still have some fears of my own to work on daily, but they are much more under control than when I had my onset some 38 years ago.

During a relapse in 2009, the shower became very bad for me. I was taking way too long to get through it. My wife Jeanine worked with me by showing me how to take a shower. Yep, she showed me like I was a kid! She videoed me doing ERP therapy that she had prescribed, and I now follow it and trust it.

"One hand glide with soap up and down any part of your body is enough," Jeanine said. "You don't have to get every single part of your body. The soap is running down anyway, and if the soap doesn't get it, the water will. If the water doesn't get it, your body is constantly producing oils to protect you. You actually don't really need so much soap like you think you do."

I made the conscious decision to trust my ERP therapy coach—Jeanine—over the OCD. Shower time varies, depending on how much I trust in any given moment. I still refer to that video from time to time for a reminder, not just of the steps but of the importance in trust.

So, what's the lesson here? Trust, then trust some more, and then act. Trusting and following directions are catalysts for healing.

Right now, try refocusing on your breath. Slow it down very gradually. If you start thinking of something else, catch yourself and bring your attention back to the breath.

# Fog Brain or Depersonalization

Some days you just feel like you are in an emotional and mental fog. I know I do. I can't quite see the light, and I wonder if there is any light. Some people call this feeling of mental cloudiness "fog brain," and some call it "depersonalization." I call it "autonomic overload." Essentially, there's just too much thought going on in your brain, and it's overloading.

But the good news is that it's not dangerous, and it will pass. Even better news is that it will pass faster if you practice mindfulness.

Right now, try refocusing on your breath. Slow it down very gradually. If you start thinking of something else, catch yourself and bring it back to the breath.

Notice what happens to your sense of presence after a while. You will see that the fog is starting to lift, and you have a new tool that works. Breath work will always bring you back to clarity. Trust that there's always light through the fog, and trust that you can bring yourself to that light with practice and patience.

Members of OCD support groups can become your extended family who understand with empathy and love.

# The Need for Family to Understand

So, why do we so desperately need our families to understand OCD? Why is it so important to us that they "get it"?

I've come to this question and conclusion about families, including my own: If you want to get better from OCD, can you look to your family for understanding and empathy? Only a little bit because they feel powerless. They don't know what to do. And they hate to see you in pain.

I think it's truly rare that a family member would really study up on your disorder. It's too hard for them, and it's too hard for us to understand it ourselves. So I don't expect my family members to understand it. They would literally have to be in my shoes.

But I do expect them to respect it and honor the courage that it takes to get better from this hidden, misunderstood disorder. And we have to be patient with them too because, if the circumstances were reversed, I think we would be just as frustrated and powerless.

Stay strong, stay respectful, and—for sure—stay loving. Then, go to a live OCD support group or join one of the many private, online OCD support groups (see "Resources" on page 189). They will become your extended family because they truly "get it."

You didn't cause this, you didn't ask for this, it's not your fault, and you are not OCD. You are you.

# It's Not Your Fault

Not much is said about guilt, but I have a black belt in it. OCD and anxiety can many times bring you to a feeling of guilt:

"Did I say something wrong?"

"Did I do something wrong?"

"I feel guilty for having this mental illness. Surely it's my fault."

I have news for you. You didn't do anything wrong. You are not to blame for any of this, and you never *ever* have to defend yourself for having OCD. Catch yourself when guilt visits or you are guilted by family or friends. You didn't cause this, you didn't ask for this, it's not your fault, and you are not OCD. You are you.

Guilt is a wasted emotion, don't you think? We all need to maintain our energy for staying present, grounded, and doing the work to get better. It's tough enough without adding unnecessary feelings of guilt.

Do the best you can under the conditions you are under. That's good enough.

# Family and Friends Can Be Your ERP Therapy Coaches

When I was dating my now wife, she knew I had OCD because I was very clear about it when we met, and I didn't want either of us to get into a relationship if there was not going to be empathy and compassion.

Jeanine has a tremendous capacity for compassion and empathy. One night, she showed me how to wash dishes by hand. I remember standing at her sink and watching and trusting her like I was a third grader. I was 46 at the time.

I watched her moves and modeled them. One wipe of soap and one rinse, then dry, and done. In a short period of time, it became no problem countering OCD and washing dishes. You see, I knew how to wash dishes, but OCD robbed me of trust and replaced it with doubt.

Family members, friends, and anyone patient enough can be your ERP therapy coach. These trusted people can teach you how to operate in life again—even in the midst of anxiety, obsessions, and compulsions—by modeling the functional behavior. I recommend that you video the modeling so you have an instant reference to go back to at any time.

When someone reminds you and shows you and educates you by example, your trust will rebuild.

To all the families out there: Take the risk to show us by example, and you'll see how strong we can be.

To the OCD sufferers: Be open to receive and be grateful.

The probability of an OCD threat being real is so low that we can safely say, "OCD *always* lies."

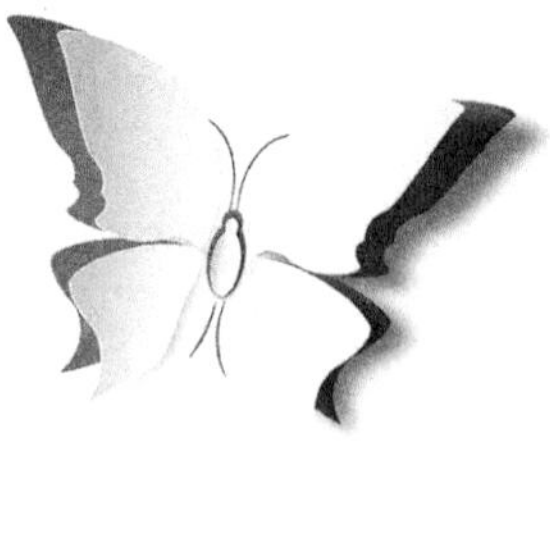

# OCD Lie vs. Real Threat

Here's basically how OCD works:

- Your mind perceives a threat of some kind.
- Your amygdala immediately fires off a fight-or-flight response.
- Anxiety starts to build.
- The perceived threat keeps looping in your thoughts and can lead to obsessions and/or compulsions in order to control the anxiety.

As you can imagine, this is a nightmare for someone with OCD. How do we differentiate between real-world threats and OCD lies?

Once I was on the off ramp of the freeway and an ambulance went flying by my car. The OCD fears hit immediately: "Could I get sick from any germs magically flying in the air from that ambulance?" No. Why? If that were true, hundreds if not thousands of cars that the ambulance drove by would all be "contaminated" too. That's an example of an OCD thought or lie.

Another day, I had to stop suddenly on the freeway to avoid hitting a car that stopped too fast. Adrenaline hit me immediately. This was a different threat. It was a real threat. My fight-or-flight response resulted in slamming on my breaks, and I avoided an accident that day.

So, what's the lesson here? Identify OCD threats as lies, and then breathe. The probability of an OCD threat being real is so low that we can safely say, "OCD *always* lies."

Once you name the lies as OCD, you are in the process and awareness of taming it before it moves into anxiety. I call this process "name it to tame it."

"Start by doing what is necessary, then do what's possible and suddenly you are doing the impossible."

— St. Francis of Assisi

# The Way over Fear

The only way over fear is not around it and not over it. We must go through it. I know it's scary, and I know it's hard. But the more we face our fears straight on and move through them, the weaker the fears become and the stronger we become.

Start by doing what is necessary for your higher good, do what's doable, and feel the feelings. The feelings of anxiety will diminish on their own once you begin to feel them. Then do what you thought was impossible because it was possible all along.

St. Francis of Assisi had a few things to say about this subject: "Start by doing what is necessary, then do what's possible and suddenly you are doing the impossible."

Affirmation: "I am willing to work to get better for my higher good."

# Daily Reprieve

All we ask for is a daily reprieve, right? Most of the time, I have to put in the work for a daily reprieve from it all. Exercise can do it, refocusing can do it, positive movies can do it, slowing down and appreciating beauty can do it, contact with people can do it, and music can definitely do it. No doubt, it's work. Tough work.

But I accept the work as part of my job to feel a little better daily. Sometimes it's just too overwhelming to achieve a daily reprieve. I always strive for it though because it's worth it.

Never doubt that momentum will build to more and more daily reprieves.

"I will take responsibility for being
aware of my pain and problems,
and caring about myself."
— Melody Beattie

# Lost in the Woods

Feeling lost in the woods? I feel that way too sometimes. It makes me feel emotionally and physically depleted, which adds to my OCD anxiety. After enough episodes of feeling this way, I realized that the depletion is a big trigger for my OCD as it correlates with my anxiety levels.

All my work these days is on reducing stress and anxiety so I don't become depleted. Self-talk, medication, meditation, rest, exercise, connection with someone, better eating, and the challenge of sleeping consistently help a lot.

These are a few pathways that work, but you don't have to take them all on at once to find your way out of the woods.

I choose peace over fear.

# Dear Anxiety

*Dear Anxiety,*

*You've been around for more than half of my life, and I've decided to finally take some real action to get you under control. Most of my friends with anxiety might not understand this action. But knowing myself—and knowing you—I believe this will be the best way to deal with your continual presence: I've decided to stop fighting you.*

*Now, that doesn't mean I'm surrendering to you either. The options of either "fight" or "surrender" are too black and white for me and too similar to your own tactics. I'm taking an approach that might throw you. After all, this is my life—not yours. So, I'm going to work with you. Not "for" or "against" but "with."*

*When you do your thing to my adrenaline, I'm not going to freak out. I'm going to calm down with soothing self-talk, meditation, slow breathing, and/or medication as directed by my doctor.*

*When you tell me that my life is a disaster, I'm not buying that thought. I will use mindfulness to stay present and grounded.*

*When you make me sweat with fear, I'm going to connect with others who feel that same anxiety and humbly ask for help.*

*When all else fails and nothing seems to work, I'm going to just feel the feelings of you because you have finite energy and you will wear out before I do.*

*So, I'm going to stop complaining about you and start handling you differently. And that's a non-negotiable fact.*

In my experience, OCD recovery is about the practice of doing something in a healthy way.

# Believing

I remember asking my main psychiatrist of 27 years about the nature of OCD. Besides the neurobiological aspect of the disorder, what is the root nature?

He basically responded, "It's not about knowing—it's about believing."

It's also about educating yourself on the disorder. That's crucial too. But once you truly want to start to break through, belief in your therapist, support group, coaches, trusted family members, and friends is vital. So, even if you know something—like washing your hands once or twice is enough—that's not quite it. You have to believe it.

And how do you believe it? I understand that this is a hard part to hear: You need to *do it*. In my experience, recovery is about doing something in a healthy way. Then, your brain starts to believe and life starts to shift for the better. Whether it is washing your hands once or twice and walking away, ignoring a horrible thought and labeling it as OCD thinking, or doing the opposite of what OCD is telling you, it's rewiring your belief system for your higher good.

Make sense? I hope so.

If you are feeling anxiety and/or panic right now ... stop, relax, breathe.

# Tips to Handle Anxiety

If you are fearful right now, if you are having anxiety right now, if you are feeling out of your body right now with overwhelm, remember this: It is not going to last.

If you refocus with music or something visual, it will help.

If you refocus on something good, it will help.

If you exercise, it will help.

If you slow down your breathing, it will help.

Even if you do nothing and ride it out, it will go away on its own. But I encourage you do the minimum, so the suffering will diminish quicker.

Hang in there. I am with you in spirit.

"Remember that underlying all our fears is a lack of trust in ourselves."

— Susan Jeffers

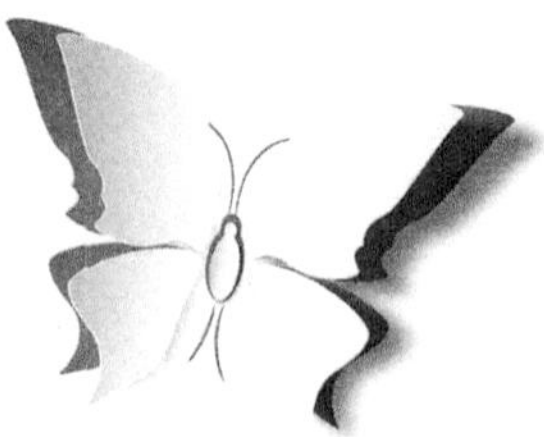

# If a Thought Doesn't Bring You Inner Peace, Don't Follow It

Here's a good slogan I heard from my wonderful therapist Sharon Davies MBACP, Director of The OCD Treatment Centre: "If a thought doesn't bring me inner peace, I don't follow it."

In my experience, two things will happen when I hear a slogan like this. Either I will kind of believe it or kind of dismiss it as some spiritual mumbo jumbo. If I go with the "dismiss it" thought, I almost immediately throw it out as a potential tool I could use to help myself. If I consider believing it, then I am setting into motion a new, healthy belief system with a new tool. So, I choose to believe this phrase.

Now, I catch myself almost every time an OCD thought comes along by asking myself, "Am I going to label this as OCD and move on—even if it persists? Or am I going to follow the thought and exacerbate the obsession even more?"

I choose to not follow OCD thoughts the best I can. This practice does get easier with time.

Taking the smallest step forward
makes you courageous.

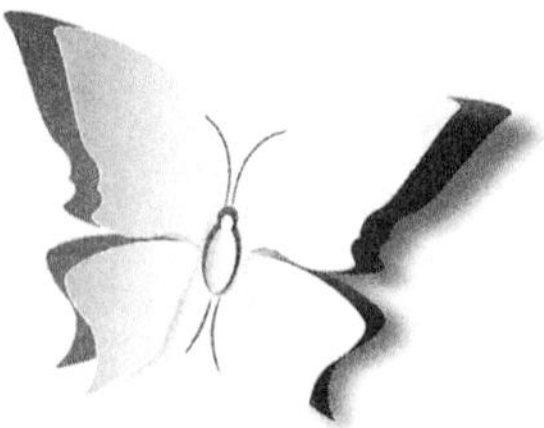

# Are You Weak or Courageous?

In my experience of talking to groups about OCD recovery, I have met extremely courageous people who deal with the disorder every day. If a family member, a teacher, an employer, a friend, or anyone else tells you differently, chalk it up to their own ignorance. If you, like me, are living with OCD, whether or not you are actively getting help, you are courageous. That is a fact.

Just getting through each day with this disorder makes you courageous.

Challenging any OCD thought makes you courageous.

Taking the smallest step forward makes you courageous.

You will get better the more you take action.

But are you weak? *Oh, please!* In this storm called OCD, I count you among the most courageous group of people I know. And that goes for all people challenged with a mental illness. This author believes in you and your ability to get better. I am inspired by your courage.

Respond to OCD with this statement:
"Thanks for sharing, but I'm not caring."

# OCD Mantras vs. Recovery Mantras

mantra: a statement or slogan repeated frequently

*OCD's mantra:* "One more time."

*Recovery's mantra:* "I'll take the risk to stop."

*OCD's mantra:* "What if?"

*Recovery's mantra:* "I don't know, so I'm going to stay in this moment."

*OCD's mantra:* "You're not going to be okay."

*Recovery's mantra:* "I can handle whatever comes my way."

*OCD's mantra:* "If you don't think this thought or do this thing, disaster is on its way."

*Recovery's mantra:* "I'll handle what life brings me because I'm stronger than I think."

*OCD's mantra:* "You have to."

*Recovery's mantra:* "Bullies don't tell me what to do."

*OCD's mantra:* "You're never going to get better."

*Recovery's mantra:* "Thanks for sharing, but I'm not caring."

You have more power, courage, and resilience in you than you think.

# You Have the Right to Refuse

Do you ever just say, "I refuse"?

I was in the shower—one of my more daily challenging places—and an OCD thought came up: "If you don't wash that arm one more time, you are going to be unclean. You have to wash again."

I recognized it as OCD and said, "Nope ... *NO* ... not going there!"

The thought came up again and again and even louder.

But so did my thoughts: "Nope ... *NO ... not going there*!"

It's a practice that takes courage and consistency to keep vigilant, just like everything else, but it helps.

You have the right to refuse.

You have the power to say, "No."

Never forget the power of music to refocus your attention and bring down anxiety.

# The Power of Refocusing

When talking about awareness, the power of refocusing can drastically lower adrenaline levels in the bloodstream. Too much adrenaline in your bloodstream means that you will have heightened anxiety, pure and simple.

And it's not so simple to bring those levels down! They will come down on their own eventually, even if you do nothing, but it can be excruciating to wait for that to happen. We all want faster relief and calmness.

As a professional nature photographer, what am I doing all the time? Almost all my focus is spent lining up the composition, making sure the subject matter is in the frame, and trying to get the light in the right spot while keeping it in focus. All this refocusing of my attention brings down my adrenaline.

I'm not suggesting that everyone take up photography, but we all need to be aware of the power of refocusing. Some refocusing tools I have used that seem to occupy my entire brain are listening to music, writing, helping someone in worse pain than I am experiencing, exercising, and using humor.

All these tools are available to you. Even in the midst of anxiety, we can become aware and refocus.

Rise above the negative thoughts with truth and facts. Even if you are not sure of all your truths and facts, your core subconscious values will weaken OCD every time.

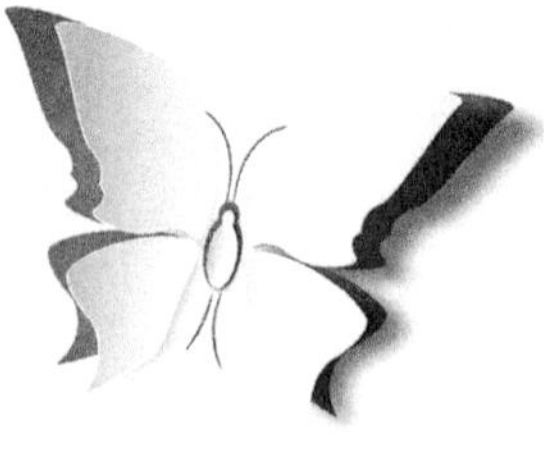

# Stop Unwanted Thoughts

How do I stop unwanted thoughts? In my experience, it's not so much about stopping thoughts because thoughts come and go nearly the entire time that we are conscious. Better to let them come and go than spend all of your energy trying to wrangle them.

I believe the best goal is rising above the thought and recognizing it for what it truly is: *a false message.* Thinking beyond the harming thought, the contamination thought, and the disturbing thought is the key to weakening it.

A common OCD thought might be that I may be harming my loved one, and this thought keeps repeating. OCD amplifies that thought in tandem with my creative imagination. Then I start growing anxious that the thought may be true.

So, how do I stop the thought? I don't stop it, but rather I breathe and rise above the thought.

I do some self-talking: "This is OCD thinking, which is always false. This is OCD trying desperately to attack my values. This is not who I am. I own my values, and I own myself. I do not intentionally harm anyone because it's not what I morally stand for. This thought is just another attempt to scare me, but I'm bigger and stronger than a thought. My thoughts are never my actions."

Rise above the thought with truth and facts. Even if you are not sure of all your truths and facts, your core subconscious values will weaken OCD every time.

You are normal. Everyone has something they deal with, and they go on anyway.

# Would You Rather ...?

Would you rather be loved or understood? I know love and understanding can go hand in hand, and many would say that being understood is being loved. But I believe that, if you have OCD or any mental illness, this question becomes vital to our trust in anyone.

Whether it be significant others, family, friends, coworkers, doctors, or therapists, I want to be understood because I know deep down that understanding has the potential to lead to real love. Understanding me as a person with OCD is paramount in creating a lasting friendship and relationship based in trust.

In turn, I want to understand those whom I relate with if they are willing to let me into their lives. Willingness is a big requirement for me. If they are not willing to understand, I'll shift my expectations and develop a different type of relationship. And that's okay. Many people just don't have the capacity to understand, and there's no judgment or shame in that awareness.

In my opinion and experience, the big picture of humanity is that everyone has something they are dealing with mentally—from OCD to depression to anxiety to stress to worry. The list is endless.

So, back to the question: Would you rather be loved or understood?

I say that trying to understand in a loving way is the answer to feeling better about yourself and feeling connected to others. Loving acceptance is the core value in any recovery.

OCD is a four-year-old bully, kicking and screaming and wanting his/her way. Be the adult in the room.

# The Four-Year-Old Bully Called OCD

Ever notice that OCD does not grow old? After being around this disorder for more than 38 years, I recognized that OCD stays the same age, and that age seems to be about four years old—a four-year-old bully always in a tantrum. Even if you are four years old, you don't have to engage with a bully. We all get older, but the obsessions and compulsions pretty much stay the same.

We become wiser, more aware, and more compassionate, but the four-year-old bully replays the same old bullying messages:

"Don't think that or you'll harm someone."

"Keep washing because all germs are bad."

"You'll get sick if you don't do what I say."

It just goes on and on. These are the same messages I was getting 38 years ago.

Now, I look at OCD as a four-year-old bully, and this new vision changes my perspective. Just the thought of a relentless bully mentally pushing me around helps me challenge OCD.

It does take practice, but we have the power to be the adult in the room.

Many times the best thing to do with OCD thoughts is just let them be and not challenge them. It takes the power out of them. Or, make them even more bizarre until you are eventually smiling at the absurdity.

# Monitoring Your OCD Thoughts

Some time ago, I had to have a root-canal procedure, and it was truly not that bad at all. But, during the preprocedure process, I was in a lot of pain, and the ol' OCD and anxiety were up and running.

I tried something different with all the bizarre, negative OCD thoughts. Instead of trying to think them away or reason them away, I consciously and deliberately put them on the shelf. I call this "monitoring OCD thoughts."

For example, "I won't be able to handle the root canal, and I'll lose my tooth and be in pain forever."

I let that thought be and mentally put it aside or on the shelf. Of course, it came back, but I stubbornly put it on the shelf again. Seemed to work really well as I started to obsess into the negative about my root canal. By monitoring my OCD thoughts, and then letting them be or putting them mentally away or whatever metaphor you want to use, I refused to follow them. And, in turn, that process kept me grounded in reality and slowed down the obsessive thinking.

The more I practiced it, the better I got at putting any OCD thought aside rather than challenging it. It seems to take the power out of it, and I felt more in control. I'm practicing this approach daily now.

BTW: The dental procedure went just fine and, as usual, none of my fears came true.

Do your best to not let an OCD
thought complete itself in your head.
Interrupt it and label it as OCD.

# Accepting the Thought as Untrue

Instead of focusing so much on making any OCD thought go away completely, what if we switched to accepting the thought as untrue? Or, at least untrue enough to work on not believing it.

Just something I'm practicing ... and it's working!

"Just do what's in front of you."
— Phil Kavanaugh

# The Most Meaningful Words I Ever Heard

One of the wisest people I have ever met in my recovery was my psychiatrist Phil. We were on a first-name basis from the time I met him in 1982 until he retired 27 years later. Phil was like a second father to me. What psychiatrist will visit you in the hospital every day you are there, including weekends? Phil did just that when I was in Therapeutic Community One for six weeks, trying to find my way to recovery from severe OCD.

Phil once said the most meaningful words to live and recover by that I have ever heard, and I use them to this day: "Jim, just do what's in front of you."

I suddenly understood that the way to challenge OCD is one obsession or compulsion at a time.

The way to calm anxiety is to stay focused on slowing down my breathing in the present.

The way to not become hypervigilant is to refocus mindfully on the present.

As gracefully as you can, do what's in front of you. Take one task at a time, one moment at a time, one step at a time.

Thank you, Phil.

Want to see someone with OCD and anxiety get better? Remind them what's right and good about them—rather than what's wrong with them.

# Words are Destructive or Healing. Your Choice.

Want to see someone with OCD decline? Remind them what's wrong with them.

Want to see them get better? Remind them what's right about them.

But it's a two-way street. We have to be aware and respect the stress OCD puts on our family members. If you are constantly looking for reassurance, then you have to stop and create boundaries with your family.

My wife Jeanine and I do it like this: She shows me how to behave, educates me, and reassures me once or twice, but then the phrase is, "Remember what I said ..."

Show this to your friends and family.

If what we think about expands—and it does—not talking about OCD for one day from time to time is a relief for you and your family and friends.

# No-OCD-Talk Days

There is something my wife and I are trying that you might be interested in trying yourself with your family and friends. But first know this: What you think about and what you talk about expand whether or not you like it. You can throw a monkey wrench into that expansion with refocus, diversion, mindfulness, and ERP therapy, which the majority of us do anyway. But there's another way to stop the expansion of OCD negativity.

We have decided from time to time to proclaim a "no-OCD-talk day." That doesn't mean I'm not going to get symptoms and work through those symptoms, but it does mean that I'm not going to talk about it for the day. I'm going to give my mind, my family, and my friends a rest from hearing me bitching about how awful it is.

If what we think about expands—and it does—not talking about OCD for one day from time to time is a relief for me and definitely for my wife, family, friends, and even people who know me at the grocery store. I'm not kidding.

We don't have to be defined by OCD because we are not OCD. We are creative, sensitive, loving, intelligent, and empathic people who deserve just as much peace in our lives as anyone else.

I'm actually going to work at doing this more often. It's all part of taking my power back.

You are not OCD. You are a person of all possibilities.

# It's All Possible

I hear that so many people want to be normal. And I get it. They want OCD under control or out of their lives. I do too. But *normal*?

Here is the definition of "normal": "conforming to a standard; usual, typical, or expected." Sounds pretty boring to me.

How about striving for "possible": "able to be done; within the power or capacity of someone or something." Sounds much more doable, logical, inviting, empowering, and fun. In my view, everything is possible. That means getting better and one day finding a cure for OCD.

Don't let OCD define who you are. Be someone who thinks and lives in possibilities.

"You can start your day over any time you want to."

— Anonymous

# Who Am I?

The words we use to define ourselves and others matter:

- "Who am I? Am I OCD or am I me?"
- "Who should I be?"
- "What should I be?"

A very talented and wise author once wrote, "I define people by who they are, not by who they were."

*Wow!* I thought to myself, "Do I define myself by who I was long ago or who I am now?"

My onset of OCD came at age 29. In the earlier years, I certainly did some things I am not proud of. I was addicted for many years, and I defined a big part of myself as secretive and shameful. For some years I tried to act like I knew things that I didn't, and I defined part of me as an imposter. And there were times I defined myself as compassionate for my acts of kindness.

For the last 38+ years, I do not define myself as OCD—*ever.* If I define myself as a fallible human, I see a compassionate, empathic person who has learned from his past, a person who wants to be better than he used to be, a person in recovery, and a person who practices living day by day in the moment, which is really the only time we have anyway.

My message to you is to not define yourself or anyone by their disability or disorder. Define yourself and others with words that lift, elevate, and encourage healing and love.

"The little things? The little moments?
They aren't little."
— Jon Kabat-Zinn

# Surfing the Wave

I believe that life is like surfing a wave. Sometimes you are down in the wave and feel you'll never get up. Then, something happens under your own momentum of courage, or a mentor helps you, and you surf to the middle of the wave for a while.

Occasionally, you'll feel on top of the wave and be grateful and relieved to be riding high, and you won't allow yourself to go to the bottom again. But then, life throws something at you, and you surf that wave the best you can with the conditions you are under.

Having OCD for 38+ years, I'm not surfing at the bottom of the wave anymore because I learned to witness the OCD and take what I call "ERP therapy risks." I have days, and moments within a day, that I feel on top of the wave and appreciate every second of it. Then there are days when I feel down on the bottom, but only for a while.

Life is a wave that we learn to ride or surf. It's up to us to stay on the board. I know it's hard—for everyone. It's not easy to surf life, so surf as gracefully as you can.

I choose to believe that we can live through any of life's waves. The waves can certainly be scary and filled with fears. However, I choose to follow these quotes from two great writers as mantras for my life:

> "You can't stop the waves, but you can learn to surf."
>
> — Jon Kabat-Zinn

> "Feel the fear and do it anyway."
>
> — Susan Jeffers

Willingness to get better is everything.
Be willing and open to recovery. You can
absolutely get better from OCD and anxiety.
How do I know this? I've been in your shoes.

# Can You Really, Truly Get Better?

The answer to this question is "yes." You can *absolutely* get better from OCD.

How do I absolutely know this? I've been in your shoes. I had extremely severe OCD when I was 29 years old. As I have mentioned throughout this book, I had no choice at that time but to be hospitalized.

Let's all face it honestly: OCD is one of the most horrible disorders that is stigmatized by the media, your friends, and your family as something that is not as bad as we who have it know that it is. I know from experience how devastating it is. And I still got better because I consciously and willingly committed to take it on. Actually, I was just too fearful that I had to be willing to get better.

So, how do I know you have good hope in getting better? You picked up this book, which is all about willingness. You are on your way—whether or not you know it.

Does it take time to get better? Yes. But, with the information and tools that are out there and with the help of a therapist, I strongly believe you can get better, depending on your willingness to practice.

Here's a word that I think applies to all of us who suffer from OCD and anxiety: equanimity (pronounced e·qua·nim·i·ty), which means "mental calmness, composure, and evenness of temper, especially in stressful situations." Its definition is something we can all strive for with our tools and anchors. We don't have to be perfect in achieving this, but at least we can try. I try daily.

# Jim's Anxiety First-Aid List

I do one or more of these things when anxiety hits:

1. Take medication, supplements, or alternative holistic approaches if appropriate, always under my doctor's care.

2. Turn on a light. Bring light to darkness in a literally physical and intentional act.

3. Do a breathing exercise. I inhale from the stomach and say, "I choose ..." and then exhale slowly while saying, "... peace." I repeat this slowly until I feel calmer.

4. Call someone or get online to a support group. A voice or message can soothe in a moment and remind me that I am not alone.

5. Refocus with music, positive movies and TV, and a safe place talking to people who do not judge you. The point here is to shift my focus away from anxiety and into the present.

6. Move a little (or a lot) or eat and drink something to shift the anxiety. I usually take a little apple as it has pectin in it, which helps my stomach. I eat or drink what helps, but I stay away from the obvious anxiety-making items like caffeine, alcohol, and sugar.

7. Do just what is in front of me. No big decisions or thoughts are allowed if I'm only focusing on what's right in front of me. Mindfully, think small. For example, if I am watching TV, then I only watch TV. I don't let my mind drift to what I need to do next. I focus intently on the characters and the story. Any time my mind drifts, I bring it right back to this one action.

8. Create a gratitude list in my mind or on paper, and the longer the list, the better. And it does not have to be big things.

For example, "I am grateful that I can breathe," "I am grateful that I have a place to live," "I am grateful that I can walk," and "I am grateful that I have a support group." This process refocuses my mind and energy for the better.

9. Trust it will pass. Anxiety is energy, and all energy passes eventually. That's a fact! If I do something about my anxiety—no matter how small—it will pass quicker.

10. Be mindful. This is a big one to calm everything down. I consciously slow down my actions and thinking. It's crucial to learn to be mindful. When I experience anxiety or panic, I mindfully become aware of it, label it as OCD, move slower, and refocus the best I can. I will then try either #3 or #7 above until I feel a shift.

11. Remind myself that, if I decide to do none of the above but simply feel the feelings, my anxiety will still calm down on its own in time.

Copy this list and paste it on your wall. Or, take a picture of this list and keep it on your phone. Keep it handy for the next time you need some words to give you steps or motivation for slowing down your anxious thinking.

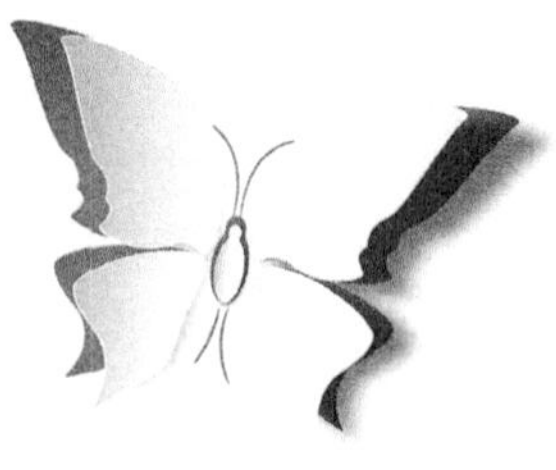

# The 7 Action Steps to Getting Better

1. *Diagnosis:* Receive a diagnosis from your family doctor or preferably a psychiatrist or qualified therapist.

2. *Acceptance:* Do what you can to accept that you have a treatable disorder and you will get better.

3. *Education:* Educate yourself as much as you can about the disorder with your healthcare worker and/or through books, videos, and helping foundations.

4. *Commitment:* Develop an attitude that you will commit to getting better. Do it for your higher good and/or your loved ones' higher good. You will get better if you commit, even a little right now.

5. *Action:* If you need medication, follow your doctor's orders. It may take some time before the medication kicks in, so be patient. If one medication does not work, be willing to try others. Remember that there is biology to this disorder, and the right meditation can truly help. You will most likely be recommended to do CBT in conjunction with ERP therapy. These are still the gold standard treatments that will get you better. Accept that the recovery process will be hard—but never *ever* as hard as suffering from OCD.

6. *Support groups:* Join an online support group. You need to be around like-minded people who understand. The members of these groups "get it" at a very high level of compassion and empathy, and they will help you.

7. *Hope:* Never *ever* give up hope because there is always hope.

# OCD References


Baer, Lee, PhD. *Getting Control: Overcoming Your Obsessions and Compulsions.* New York: Plume, 2012.

Callner, James. *It's a Matter of Trust: Hope & Solutions for OCD and How I Got Better.* Aptos, CA: James Callner, 2016.

Grayson, Jonathan. *Freedom from Obsessive Compulsive Disorder: A Personalized Recovery Program for Living with Uncertainty,* Updated Edition. New York: Berkley, 2014.

Hershfield, Jon, MFT, Tom Corboy, MFT, et al. *The Mindfulness Workbook for OCD: A Guide to Overcoming Obsessions and Compulsions Using Mindfulness and Cognitive Behavioral Therapy (A New Harbinger Self-Help Workbook),* Second Edition. Oakland, CA: New Harbinger Publications, 2020.

Hyman, Bruce M., PhD, LCSW, and Cherlene Pedrick, RN. *OCD Workbook: Your Guide to Breaking Free from Obsessive-Compulsive Disorder (A New Harbinger Self-Help Workbook),* 3rd Edition. Oakland, CA: New Harbinger Publications, 2010.

Schwartz, Jeffrey M. and Rebecca Gladding, MD. *You Are Not Your Brain: The 4-Step Solution for Changing Bad Habits, Ending Unhealthy Thinking, and Taking Control of Your Life.* New York: Abery Publishing, 2012.

Tolle, Eckhart. *The Power of Now: A Guide to Spiritual Enlightenment.* Vancouver: Namaste Publishing, 2004.

# Resources

*Foundations*

Anxiety and Depression Association of America
BeyondOCD.org
International OCD Foundation
National Alliance on Mental Illness
Peace of Mind Foundation, Inc.

*Videos on YouTube*

Katie d'Ath (OCD coaching videos)
OCDCoachingVideos.com
Jeffrey Schwartz (OCD psychiatrist and educator)

*Facebook Private Online Support Groups (all free to join)*

These are just some of the Facebook private OCD support groups that I suggest you join for anytime support. Other online platforms have more OCD support groups, but these are the ones I am involved in on Facebook:

Anxiety and Depression Support Group
Obsessive Compulsive Disorder (OCD) sufferers' friendship and support group
OCD & Anxiety Recovery Coach
OCD/Mental Health Awareness International
OCD Friends
OCD Only, Support group
Support 4 Everything OCD

Printed in Great Britain
by Amazon

16392316R00108